Homes

Written by Matt Ralphs

Collins

We live in all sorts of homes.

2

3

Some homes are high up.

Some homes are noisy.

Some homes are quiet.

Some homes float on water.

Some homes have wheels.

12

Different homes

 Ideas for reading

Written by Clare Dowdall, PhD
Lecturer and Primary Literacy Consultant

Reading objectives:
- read and understand simple sentences
- use phonic knowledge to decode regular words and read them aloud accurately
- demonstrate understanding when talking with others about what they have read

Communication and language objectives:
- listen attentively in a range of situations
- listen to stories, accurately anticipating key events and respond to what they hear with relevant comments, questions or actions
- express themselves effectively, showing awareness of listeners' needs
- develop their own narratives and explanations by connecting ideas or events

Curriculum links: Understanding the world

High frequency words: what, of, do, you, in, we, all, of, some, are, have

Interest words: homes, high, noisy, quiet, float, wheels

Resources: sticky notes, magazines with pictures of houses and homes, pencils and paper

Word count: 29

Build a context for reading

- Ask children what you normally find in a home. Make a list of what homes usually have, e.g. a door, a bed, windows. Display the list for the children to see and use later.
- Look at the front cover together. Ask children whether they would like to have a boat as a home. Read the title and the blurb, pointing to each word as you read and encouraging the children to join in.
- Discuss the question asked in the blurb, *What sort of home do you live in?*, and ask children to describe the home they live in.

Understand and apply reading strategies

- Turn to pp2–3. Read the text together. Dwell on the word *homes*, and check that children can read the word.
- Turn to pp4–5. Model how to retrieve information from the images by wondering aloud, e.g. *I wonder what it would be like to live in a tall home*. Look at the word *high*. Remind children of the range of strategies that they can use to read the word, e.g. phonics or clues in the picture.